3 4028 08811 4450
HARRIS COUNTY PUBLIC LIBRARY

J 799.215 He
Hemstock, Ar
Bow hunting   W9-ALJ-793

$10.00
ocn868429204
First edition.   08/03/2015

Bow Hunting

Annie Wendt Hemstock

PowerKiDS press
New York

Open Season

Published in 2015 by The Rosen Publishing Group, Inc.
29 East 21st Street, New York, NY 10010

Copyright © 2015 by The Rosen Publishing Group, Inc.

All rights reserved. No part of this book may be reproduced in any form without permission in writing from the publisher, except by a reviewer.

First Edition

Editor: Amelie von Zumbusch
Book Design: Greg Tucker
Book Layout: Joe Carney
Photo Research: Katie Stryker

Photo Credits: Cover, p. 4 Shane W Thompson/Shutterstock.com; p. 5 DEA/M. FANTIN/De Agostini/Getty Images; pp. 6, 7 Tom Reichner/Shutterstock.com; p. 8 Fuse/Thinkstock; pp. 11, 29 Nate Allred/Shutterstock.com; p. 12 marcovarro/Shutterstock.com; p. 15 Michael Olsen/iStock/Thinkstock; p. 17 Marcel Jancovic/Shutterstock.com; p. 18 Igor Zhorov/iStock/Thinkstock; p. 19 Stanislav Komogorov/Shutterstock.com; p. 20 Michael Mill/iStock/Thinkstock; p. 21 Keith Publicover/Shutterstock.com; p. 22 Comstock/ Stockbyte/Thinkstock; p. 25 Jeff Banke/Shutterstock.com; p. 26 groden/iStock/Thinkstock; p. 27 Novastock/Photolibrary/Getty Images.

Library of Congress Cataloging-in-Publication Data

Hemstock, Annie Wendt, author.
Bow hunting / by Annie Wendt Hemstock. — First edition.
    pages cm. — (Open season)
Includes index.
ISBN 978-1-4777-6715-3 (library binding) — ISBN 978-1-4777-6716-0 (pbk.) — ISBN 978-1-4777-6717-7 (6-pack)
1. Bowhunting—Juvenile literature. I. Title.
SK36.H435 2015
799.2'15—dc23
                                    2014000309

Manufactured in the United States of America

CPSIA Compliance Information: Batch #WS14PK3: For Further Information contact Rosen Publishing, New York, New York at 1-800-237-9932

Contents

An Ancient Invention

Nobody knows who invented the first bow and arrow because it happened so long ago. We do know that they were important inventions. A hunter with a bow and arrow did not have to get as close to his prey. That meant he had a better chance of surviving.

This young archer enjoys the challenge of hunting with a bow.

Ancient cave paintings like this one prove that bow hunters have been around for thousands of years.

When firearms were invented, many people stopped hunting with bows. Some people, though, like the challenge of bow hunting. They like having to get close to their prey. They like how quiet a bow is compared to a gun. They believe that hunting with a bow is more sporting than with a gun because an animal has a better chance to get away. They take pride in becoming skilled at archery, the sport of using a bow and arrow.

Game Galore

There are many kinds of **game** animals. Deer, elk, moose, and bears are called big game. Bison, mountain goats, and caribou are also big game. There are more than 20 **species** of big-game animals in North America. All of them have been hunted with bows and arrows.

There are even more kinds of small game. Because of their size, small-game animals are much harder to hunt with a bow. Squirrels and rabbits are popular **quarry**.

Big game like this deer present a big challenge for bow hunters.

Hunting Facts

Have you ever thought of fishing with a bow and arrow? Bow fishing is becoming more popular. Rough fish, like carp, are the most common fish taken with a bow.

Wild turkeys are among the most popular game birds for bow hunting.

Wild turkeys are a challenging target for bow hunters. Other game birds, like pheasant, are, too. Make sure to check the laws in your area. You may be surprised at how many animals and birds you can hunt with your bow.

One of the reasons people hunt with bows is because it is a challenge. An arrow has less power than a bullet. It also has a much shorter **range**. In order to make a quick, clean kill, you must get much closer to your prey.

Bow hunters get close to animals in different ways. Before the **hunting season** starts, good hunters spend time in the woods. They learn where animals spend their time. This is called scouting. Scouting can help you figure out the best places to hunt and the best ways to get close to your quarry.

Sometimes hunters sit very still and wait for their prey to come close to them. Other times, bow hunters will stalk their prey by moving very carefully and quietly.

Bow hunting is often more challenging than hunting with firearms. This hunter must get much closer to his prey in order to take a clean shot.

There are several ways to make bow hunting a little easier. **Camouflage** clothing helps you blend in with the area around you. These clothes might look like leaves, bark, or grass. There is even camouflage that looks like snow. Hunting bows are often covered with camouflage patterns, too.

Bow hunters sometimes use a **blind**. Other times, they will hunt from a platform in a tree. This is called a stand. Animals do not often look for danger from above. They are less likely to notice a hunter in a tree stand.

The different-colored splotches that make up camouflage break up the outline of the wearer. The colors themselves blend in with the colors of the surrounding landscape.

10

Most bow hunters try to keep their prey from smelling them. They use different scents to cover human odors. They also stand so that the wind does not blow their scent toward their prey.

Bows and More Bows

Some people like to hunt with traditional bows. These hunters choose longbows or recurve bows. These are the simplest bows. With recurves and longbows, the farther back you pull the bowstring, the more energy it takes. You have to be very strong to hunt with them. If you have to hold your bow at **full draw** while you wait for a good shot, you can get very tired.

Longbows like this one require strong arms and steady aim.

Compound bows and crossbows are more complex. However, you do not have to use as much energy to hold back their bowstrings. This means they can have higher draw weights and more power. In some states, you have to have special permission to hunt with a crossbow.

Hunting Facts

The distance you pull the bowstring back to shoot is the draw length. The amount of energy it takes to pull the string back is the draw weight.

Compound Bows

The body of a compound bow is the riser. The part you hold is the grip. Above the grip are the arrow rest and the sight. On each end of the riser are the limbs. These limbs bend when you draw the bow. A compound bow has cables and special pulleys called cams. When you draw the bowstring, the cams turn, and the amount of energy you need to hold the string goes down. This is called let-off.

This modern compound bow has cams and pulleys that make it easier to shoot farther and hunt big game.

Compound bows are the most popular for all kinds of hunting. The let-off makes it easier to wait for a good shot. It also makes it easier to use a compound bow with a high draw weight. This is important for hunting big game.

To shoot your bow, place an arrow on your bowstring. The **shaft** sits on the rest. Your bow shoulder should face the target. Place your feet shoulder width apart. Hold the grip loosely in your hand. Holding it tightly can make you miss your shot.

Place the first three fingers of your other hand on the bowstring. With the bow pointing toward your target, bring your bow to shoulder height. Pull back the bowstring until it is near the corner of your mouth. Hold your hand firmly against your face.

This hunter has placed the arrow's shaft against the rest and has drawn back the bowstring. He is ready to aim and fire.

Bring your sight in line with the spot you want to hit. Relax the fingers on the string while keeping your sight on the target. Do not drop your bow arm until the arrow hits.

Hunting Facts

Always have an arrow on the bowstring before drawing it back. Releasing a bowstring without an arrow is called a dry fire. This is very dangerous and can damage a bow.

Crossbows

Crossbows are quite different from other kinds of bows. A crossbow has a **stock** that you hold to your shoulder, the same way you would hold a rifle. The limbs and riser are attached to the sides of the stock. On the far end, away from the stock, is the stirrup. To draw back, or cock, the string, you put your foot in the stirrup. It is much harder to draw back a crossbow string, so many hunters use a **cocking aid**.

A crossbow is almost like a rifle that launches arrows. You hold the stock against your shoulder and pull the trigger in order to shoot.

The crossbow hunting season is often more limited than the season for hunting with other kinds of bows.

You do not have to use your muscles to hold back the string once it is cocked. A lever holds the string in place until you are ready to shoot. To shoot a crossbow, you pull a trigger like the trigger on a gun.

Straight as an Arrow

At one time, arrows were made of wood. Wooden arrows should be used only with recurves or longbows. It is dangerous to shoot wooden arrows with a compound bow. Today, most arrows are made of aluminum or carbon. They can be used with compound bows, recurves, and longbows. Arrows for crossbows are often called bolts.

Arrows and broadheads come in different shapes and sizes. Make sure you use the right arrow for your bow and the right broadhead for the game you are hunting.

Hunting Facts

Broadheads are the most common arrowheads for hunting. There are also special tips for hunting small game. Make sure to choose the right arrowheads for the game you hunt.

If you are hunting a large quarry, such as an elk, you will need to use heavier arrows than you would to hunt smaller game.

Aluminum arrows cost less, but they can bend. Carbon arrows are lighter and sturdier. They will flex but not bend. They can also go faster. Carbon arrows can shatter if they are damaged. Always check your arrows for cracks or nicks before shooting.

Make sure the arrows you use are matched to your bow. The wrong arrows will not fly as well. They could also damage your bow.

Gear Up

There are many kinds of gear that can help you be a successful bow hunter. Arrow rests made for bow hunting will keep your arrow in place while you hunt. Sights will help you aim accurately. Some sights have pins that glow so they are easier to see. Many hunters use release aids to draw and fire their bows. These releases help you shoot more accurately. **Stabilizers** help you hold steady at full draw.

This hunter's bow is equipped with a stabilizer that helps him hold the bow steady while he aims and draws.

An arrow holder, or quiver, will keep your arrows close until you are ready to shoot. A hunting quiver will also protect the blades of your broadheads. A case will keep your bow and gear safe and in good shape. You can find cases made of soft fabric or hard plastic.

Be a Safe and Legal Hunter

Every state has hunting laws. You may need a **license** before you hunt. In some states, you need to pass a bow hunter safety class. You will need to know when the bow hunting season starts and ends. In many areas, the seasons for bow hunting are longer than the seasons for hunting with guns. The number of animals you can legally kill is the bag limit. Make sure you know the laws for the areas in which you plan to hunt.

For some kinds of game, there are laws that tell you what draw weight your bow must have. If your bow has a draw weight that is too low, your arrow will not have enough power. You won't be able to make a good killing shot.

This hunter killed his bag limit of one deer. Make sure you know the bag limit of any animal you plan to hunt in your state.

Good hunters try to make sure that the animals they hunt do not suffer. It is important to know the best place to aim for a killing shot. It is also important to know how far away the animal is. The distance to your quarry will affect where you aim. It is your responsibility to make a shot that will kill, not just wound.

Good hunters practice archery as much as possible. It is important to be an expert shot so that game animals are killed quickly and do not suffer.

Practice until you can shoot your bow well. Then, practice as if you were hunting. Wear the same clothes you will wear hunting. If you will be hunting from a tree stand, practice from a stand. Practice with your hunting arrows. Develop a good sense of how far away things are. The best way to become a good bow hunter is to practice.

If you plan to hunt from a tree stand, spend time sitting in it to make sure you will be comfortable there. Remember, there are several kinds of tree stands.

A Hard–Won Reward

Bow hunting is challenging. It takes a lot of effort to become a good shot with a bow and arrow. It is not easy to get close to wild animals. You have to be very quiet and stealthy. Knowing how far away something is can be tricky. It is not easy to make that perfect shot, especially when you are excited.

Bow hunting is an enjoyable challenge that allows you to spend time outside and teaches you to be as silent as the animals you hunt.

Hunting with a bow and arrow is also very rewarding. You put all of your skills to the test. You feel like you are a part of the natural world. When your hunt is successful, you know that it was worth all of your hard work.

Happy Hunting

⊕ Make sure your bow fits you well. It should have the right draw weight and draw length.

⊕ Always use arrows that are made to match your bow and each other.

⊕ Always check your bowstring, cables, and arrows before you shoot. If they are damaged, they need to be replaced.

⊕ Make sure your broadheads are razor sharp. Dull broadheads will not do a good job. Handle them carefully so you do not get cut!

⊕ Before you hunt, practice with your broadheads so you know your arrows will fly well with them.

⊕ Always be aware of what is behind your target in case you miss or your arrow passes through.

⊕ When adjusting your sight, move it in the same direction the arrow hits. If the arrow hits high, move the sight higher. If it hits right, move the sight to the right.

⊕ Most bow hunting injuries come from falling off tree stands. Wear a safety harness.

Glossary

blind (BLYND) A place where people hide to watch or shoot animals.

camouflage (KA-muh-flahj) Having a color or shape that matches what is around something and helps hide it.

cocking aid (KO-king AYD) A device that makes it easier to load a crossbow.

full draw (FUL DRAW) A position in which a bow's string is drawn and ready to shoot.

game (GAYM) Wild animals that are hunted for food.

hunting season (HUN-ting SEE-zun) The time during which it is legal to hunt a certain kind of animal.

license (LY-suns) Official permission to do something.

quarry (KWOR-ee) Something that is being hunted.

range (RAYNJ) The distance something can travel.

shaft (SHAFT) A cylindrical bar.

species (SPEE-sheez) Kinds of living things. All people are one species.

stabilizers (STAY-buh-ly-zerz) Weights that make it easier to hold a bow steady while shooting.

stock (STOK) The part of a gun or crossbow that you hold against your shoulder to fire it.

Harris County Public Library
Houston, Texas

Index

Websites

Due to the changing nature of Internet links, PowerKids Press has developed an online list of websites related to the subject of this book. This site is updated regularly. Please use this link to access the list: www.powerkidslinks.com/os/bow/